Writing Mysteries, Movies, Monster Stories, and More

NANCY BENTLEY AND DONNA GUTHRIE

ILLUSTRATED BY JEREMY TUGEAU

THE MILLBROOK PRESS
BROOKFIELD, CONNECTICUT

To Nick and Rachael, future writers—N.B.
To Amanda and Megan—D.W.G.

Library of Congress Cataloging-in-Publication Data
Bentley, Nancy.
Writing mysteries, movies, monster stories, and more /
Nancy Bentley and Donna Guthrie; illustrated by Jeremy Tugeau.
p. cm.
Includes bibliographical references and index.
ISBN 0-7613-1452-0 (lib. bdg.)
1. Authorship. 2. Literary form. I. Guthrie, Donna.
II. Tugeau, Jeremy, ill. III. Title.
PN147.B475   2001
808'.02—dc21   00-056222

Published by The Millbrook Press, Inc.
2 Old New Milford Road
Brookfield, Connecticut 06804
www.millbrookpress.com

CONTENTS

Are You a Writer?

Ou love to read and you love to write. Have you ever thought about publishing your stories? Ask yourself these questions: Can you work independently? Can you find time to write? Can you finish a project? Can you take rejection and still keep trying? If you answer "yes" to these questions, you've got what it takes to be a writer.

Writers like Stephen King, John Grisham, and J. K. Rowling were once kids like you with

(5)

plenty of ideas for stories and the desire to have them published. Today Stephen King writes books and stories dripping with horror. John Grisham's mystery novels are filled with suspense. And J. K. Rowling's books about Harry Potter transport us into a world of humor and fantasy. Each of these authors writes for a specific fiction *genre*. "Genre" (ZHON-ra) is a French word that means "category" or "kind."

GENRE WRITING

Genre fiction is a term used in the publishing industry to describe popular novels, such as mystery, fantasy, and science fiction. Each genre has its own rules, guidelines, and a loyal reading audience. Publishers appreciate these readers and are always looking for writers who can write these types of stories. If you can write mysteries, science fiction, fantasy, or humor, you'll have an easier time getting published.

The next big question is what kind of writing do you want to do? The answer may be found in your own room. Look around. What kinds of books and magazines do you see? Humor? Fantasy? Science fiction? Mysteries? Movies? It's easiest to write what you like to read.

This book will show you how to write and publish your genre stories in magazines, in school literary journals, and in the world of online publishing and electronic media.

All writers are interested in people. They pay attention to details, listen to conversations, and wonder what motivates people to do the things they do.

Writers enjoy playing with language and the rhythm and flow of words. Authors know there is power in writing and like to use it to express their feelings and to influence people.

Good writers know that writing is a daily routine and not a one-time inspiration. Successful writers write everywhere, under all conditions, from noisy lunchrooms to quiet study halls. No excuses.

Writing can be a solitary pursuit. As a writer, you may work in the quiet of your room, away from crowds and the noisy world. Loneliness is often the biggest complaint of beginning writers.

Time for writing comes in bits and pieces. Catch bits of time during the day to plan or think about your writing. When you're traveling to and from school, waiting for a ride, or before going to bed at night, use these moments of time to jot down that idea that just won't go away.

And like any new skill, writing takes practice. It must be something you do every day. Carry a small notebook for collecting story ideas, jotting down conversations, and describing the places and people you see every day. Practice using new words and phrases to describe the ordinary.

Writing is like running a marathon. You can't start out running twenty-six miles. Strength and endurance come from running a little more each day. Don't expect to begin by writing a novel. Set realistic goals, which may mean completing three pages of a short story.

Good writing means rewriting. After you've completed a rough draft, the polishing begins. You're writing on paper, not cement; anything can be changed. Learn to enjoy reworking even your favorite words.

Successful writers live with criticism and rejection. Share your stories with people you trust. Listen to their opinions—then weigh them against the story you want to write.

Look for the writing exercises in every chapter of this book. Use them to sharpen your writing skills and become a better writer.

WRITING EXERCISES

1. Write a paragraph about each member of your family.
2. Describe a time in your life when you tried something and failed. What did you do then?
3. Tell about a book that you have read more than once and would recommend.
4. What is the first story you ever heard? Can you retell it?
5. Listen to two of your friends talking. Write down everything they say.

CHAPTER 1

Fiction

THE BIG STORY

A genre is a type of fiction. The word *fiction* comes from a Latin word meaning "to make," "to form," and sometimes "to feign" or "pretend." Unlike nonfiction, which answers the questions "who," "what," "when," "where," "why," and "how" with factual information, fiction is an invented world filled with imaginary characters, places, and events that the reader comes to believe as real.

Beginning writers sometimes think that every story has already been told. Your challenge is to take an old idea and make it new again through your own perceptions and experiences.

We all know stories about a hero who faces obstacles and trials to overcome evil and save the world. This character has been used again and again. But this didn't stop George Lucas from creating Luke Skywalker and the *Star Wars* adventures. It was George Lucas's unique telling that made the story different.

Classic story ideas and characters will change when they reflect your time and place in the world. No one else can write them but you.

Ideas, characters, point of view, dialogue, plot, scene, and theme combine to make good fiction. These are the elements of fiction.

IDEAS

Where can you find ideas for stories? Ideas come from traveling around the world or walking around the block, watching television news or listening to school gossip, worrying about moving to a new town, or losing a best friend. Look for interesting people and unusual situations, because the two most important things in a story are characters and plot.

CHARACTERS

Characters are the most important element of a story. Strong characters capture readers and pull them into an imaginary world. First impressions are important.

Readers must identify with the main character from the moment he or she appears on the page. This main character is the hero of the story and is called the **protagonist**.

The villain, or **antagonist**, is the character who works against or is in conflict with the hero. He or she interferes with the protagonist's wishes, goals, or actions.

In fiction there are also **supporting characters** that can add flavor and depth to the story. They include the main character's best friend or little sister, the villain's sidekick, or a spiteful girlfriend.

Too often new authors use people from real life without changing them. Instead of writing about someone you know (which would be nonfiction), choose one or two characteristics that make your person more interesting, quirky, and worth reading about.

Never use stereotypes. A **stereotype** is a pattern or form that doesn't change. A character that is a stereotype fits a mold of a particular type of person. The "dumb blonde," "jock," and "computer geek" are fine for the comics but not for fiction because they are too predictable.

Good writing requires more than stereotypes. Explore the surprises and contradictions that exist in everyone. Real people are not all good or all bad; they're brave one moment and cowardly the next. Use your imagination and insights to make the blonde, jock, and geek three-dimensional, real people.

Make all your characters authentic by putting them into realistic and challenging situations. Give them a physical body, inner thoughts, and a history of how they relate to and interact with others.

Physical description. You must know exactly what the main character looks like. Clip out photographs from magazines or write a description. Paste these into your note-book and use them for inspiration. Focus on just one or two physical attributes and describe them well. Perhaps your computer geek could have bulging biceps and wear designer glasses.

Thoughts. Everyone has an inner life with memories, ideas, feelings, and emotions. In your notebook, write a page from your character's most private diary to reveal a dream, a fear, or a secret that no one knows. This would be a good place to let your jock write a sonnet. You may not use all this information in your story, but it will help you understand your character and his or her motivations.

History. Is your character an orphan or part of a large family? Is he the oldest or the youngest child? Is he rich, poor, or middle-class? Educated or illiterate? Where does he live? These facts woven together create the fabric of your character's life. They are the parameters and boundaries of his experiences and his world. If your computer savvy character lives in Alaska instead of California's Silicon Valley, his world and the people in it will be very different.

POINT OF VIEW

Once you have a main character firmly in mind, you can decide the point of view of your story. The point of view determines how the reader sees the story: up close or on the sidelines, against the ropes feeling the punches or outside the ring. Point of view can be single or first-person, third-person, omniscient, or multiple.

Single or first-person viewpoint sees the story through the eyes of a single character and uses the pronoun "I." The advantage of using first-person point of view is that you as the writer feel close to the action because you are inside the character's mind. The disadvantage is that you can write only what the viewpoint character sees, feels, and thinks. How would you tell the reader what other characters are thinking or doing? This information must come to the viewpoint character through description, dialogue, and interaction with others.

I always knew my grandmother was a strong woman, but I didn't realize how strong until the summer of the big flood when she saved my life.

Usually the viewpoint character is the protagonist. The reader sees the story through the hero's eyes. Readers identify with the viewpoint character because he or she has the most to lose or gain.

Sometimes genre writers will use a supporting character to tell the story. In the mystery series *The Tales of Sherlock Holmes*, Doctor Watson is the viewpoint character. He, like the reader, waits for the great detective to reveal the clues one by one. The viewpoint character can be a sidekick, best friend, or family member.

Third-person viewpoint. In this method, you the writer tell the story from the main character's point of view. The ***narration***, or how the story is told, refers to the main character as "he" or "she."

Lizzie watched her grandmother slowly wash the last of the breakfast dishes. "Grandma, the water's rising," Lizzie said. "We've got to get out!"

Omniscient viewpoint lets the writer tell the story from a distance. It is often used in novels filled with many characters. With the omniscient viewpoint, the writer is able to be inside several characters and reveal feelings, actions, and motivations. Using this viewpoint, the author can explain, instruct, and interpret ideas about society, history, and culture.

The icy black water seeped beneath the cabin door. Grandma touched the gold locket that hung around her neck. If she could hold on to this, everything would be okay. Lizzie reached for the lantern. The matches were damp and wouldn't light. She was afraid. They would have to make the journey in the dark.

Multiple viewpoint shows the story from the eyes of two or more characters. Chapter by chapter, each character takes turns telling the story from the first-person point of view.

When I saw the water seeping through the door, I tried to pretend I wasn't afraid. Oh sure, things take a little longer at the age of eighty-six. I don't hear or see that well. And sometimes the people I know and the places I've been get all mixed up in my mind. But even an old woman like me knew we were in trouble.

I knew by the look on Gram's face that she was pretending she didn't see the water seeping under the door. Fear slowed her down. Her steps were small

and she took a long time clearing the dishes. But I could hear the sound of the
storm, and I knew that the dam three miles upriver was going to break.

DIALOGUE

Dialogue happens when two characters talk to each other. When conversation is written down it is called dialogue. In real life, everyday small talk and social pleasantries, such as "Hi, how's it going?" or "I'm fine, how are you?" are necessary. In fiction, this kind of conversation is boring. Dialogue must have a purpose. It should do one of three things: reveal something about the character, move the plot along, or create tension.

"Excuse me, Captain, this spaceship is no longer under your command. I'm in charge now."

The above dialogue shows an assertive character, a change in events, and tension. Not all three things have to happen at once, but every word should count. Listen to ordinary speech and write it down. Notice the breaks and pauses in people's conversations and how they often repeat themselves. Now rewrite the conversation as interesting dialogue. Read it aloud to hear how it sounds.

PLOT

Once you decide the point of view from which your story will be told, begin to plot your story. **Plot** is a series of cause-and-effect sit-

uations that creates a pattern of action and reaction. The plot is the structure of the story.

Even the simplest story has a beginning, a middle, and an end. In the beginning you meet the main character and learn about her goals and the obstacles she will have to overcome to achieve them. In the middle the main character faces the obstacles. The end contains the **climax**, or the most exciting point in the story. **Resolution** comes when the obstacles are overcome and everything is explained.

You may choose to outline or plan your story from beginning to end, or let the characters and their problems move the story along as you write it. Most writers use a combination of these two strategies.

Another way to think of the **plot** is as a road map to help your character travel through the story. Plot involves the reader in the game of "why." Why does a character think, feel, or act the way he does? Plot helps the reader to remember what has already happened in order to project the outcome.

To make the trip exciting, your character must encounter potholes and roadblocks along the way. These detours can be problems, challenges, or conflicts with other characters. These build tension and interest.

These critical decisions are sometimes called **plot points** because the character makes a decision that alters the course of the story. There are usually two plot points in any story. One comes between the beginning and the middle of the story and the other at the climax.

For example, Chris, a young athlete wants to impress his busy father by making the football team. Chris chooses to take steroids

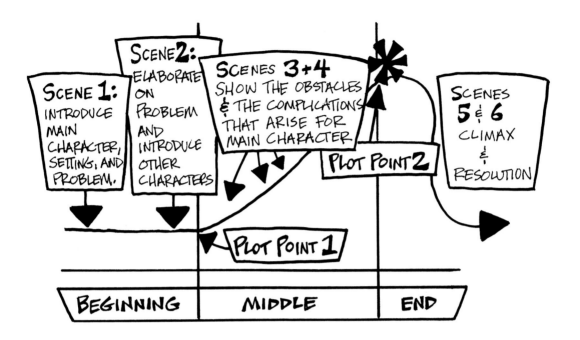

SCENE 1: INTRODUCE MAIN CHARACTER, SETTING, AND PROBLEM.

SCENE 2: ELABORATE ON PROBLEM AND INTRODUCE OTHER CHARACTERS

SCENES 3+4 SHOW THE OBSTACLES & THE COMPLICATIONS THAT ARISE FOR MAIN CHARACTER

PLOT POINT 2

SCENES 5 & 6 CLIMAX & RESOLUTION

PLOT POINT 1

BEGINNING   MIDDLE   END

without the coach's or his father's knowledge. After a few weeks, he begins to have health problems. His best friend accuses him of illegal drug use and wants him to stop. At the big game, Chris collapses on the football field. In the hospital he confesses everything to his father and the coach. Chris is suspended from the team but learns how much his father loves him.

Beginning: Chris wants his father's love and respect.

Plot Point #1:   Chris decides to take steroids in order to stay on the football team.

Middle:	He begins to have health complications. The coach questions Chris about the changes in his strength and physique. Chris lies and says he is not using steroids. His best friend learns the truth.
Plot Point #2:	Chris's friend warns him not to play in the game. Chris decides to play.
Climax:	Chris collapses on the field. At the hospital he tells his father and the coach the truth.
End:	Chris is suspended from the team but comes to realize how much his father loves him.

SCENE

Plots are made up of many scenes. A **scene** is a unit of dramatic action that introduces change or potential change. It takes place in a specific time or setting. In the story of the young athlete, one scene might be between Chris and his busy father in the car on the way to school. In actual writing, a scene can be just two or three paragraphs. A series of scenes arranged in a logical dramatic sequence creates a story.

Every scene must show action. Something has to happen. Characters have goals they want to achieve. As they try to reach their goals, they are blocked by others, by the environment, or by their own limitations. Trying to overcome those obstacles puts characters in **conflict**. There are five basic types of conflict: characters against themselves, characters against other characters, and characters against nature, society, and fate. Conflict can be either internal or external. An example of internal conflict is Chris's fear of not being strong enough to play on the team. External conflict occurs when the coach confronts him about possible drug use.

The purpose of each scene should be to advance the plot. As you create a scene, ask yourself these questions:

> Why do I need this scene?
> Who are the characters?
> What is the conflict?
> Where does the scene take place?
> When does the scene happen?
> How does the scene end?

THEME

Once the problem is solved, the character changes. This change illustrates the **theme** of the story. The theme in the young athlete story is the love between a father and son. While a plot is the series of events that happen in a story, a theme is the larger underlying idea such as love, honesty, jealousy, or world peace.

WHAT'S YOUR **THEME?**   WHAT'S YOUR **PLOT?**

1. **A *dull beginning*.** Jump into the story and make something happen. Hook your reader with the very first line.

   > *Mac knew that he was in trouble when he saw the flashing lights. He threw the can of spray paint into the bushes. He'd try the truth but his paint-splattered T-shirt was going to be hard to explain.*

2. **Problems with dialogue:** either too much or too little, or the overuse of slang and dialect. **Dialect** is the language of a particular region, social class, or ethnic group. Use dialogue to show action and move the story along.

> *"Martin, I know you were there last night."*
>
> *"Stay out of this, man," he said. "It ain't your business."*
>
> *"Since I'm the one they caught, it is my business."*

3. **Plot problems** caused by missing information that you know but forget to tell the reader or by including too many coincidences that make your story unbelievable.

4. **An unsatisfactory ending** because there's no deeper theme to the story. Readers need a good cry or a good belly laugh. Don't let your reader down at the end by writing, "It was all just a dream."

WRITING EXERCISES

1. In your notebook write a description of a character based on someone you know. Give him or her a physical body and inner thoughts, and describe how your character relates to other people.

2. Practice point of view by writing one paragraph in single viewpoint and one in third person.

3. Write the beginning of a short story in which the main character's problem is revealed in the first two paragraphs.

4. Watch your favorite television sitcom. Write down the main character, his or her problem, and the obstacles that stand in the way of solving it.

5. Write examples of dialogue using a member of your family and your best friend. Read them aloud to see if the people can recognize themselves.

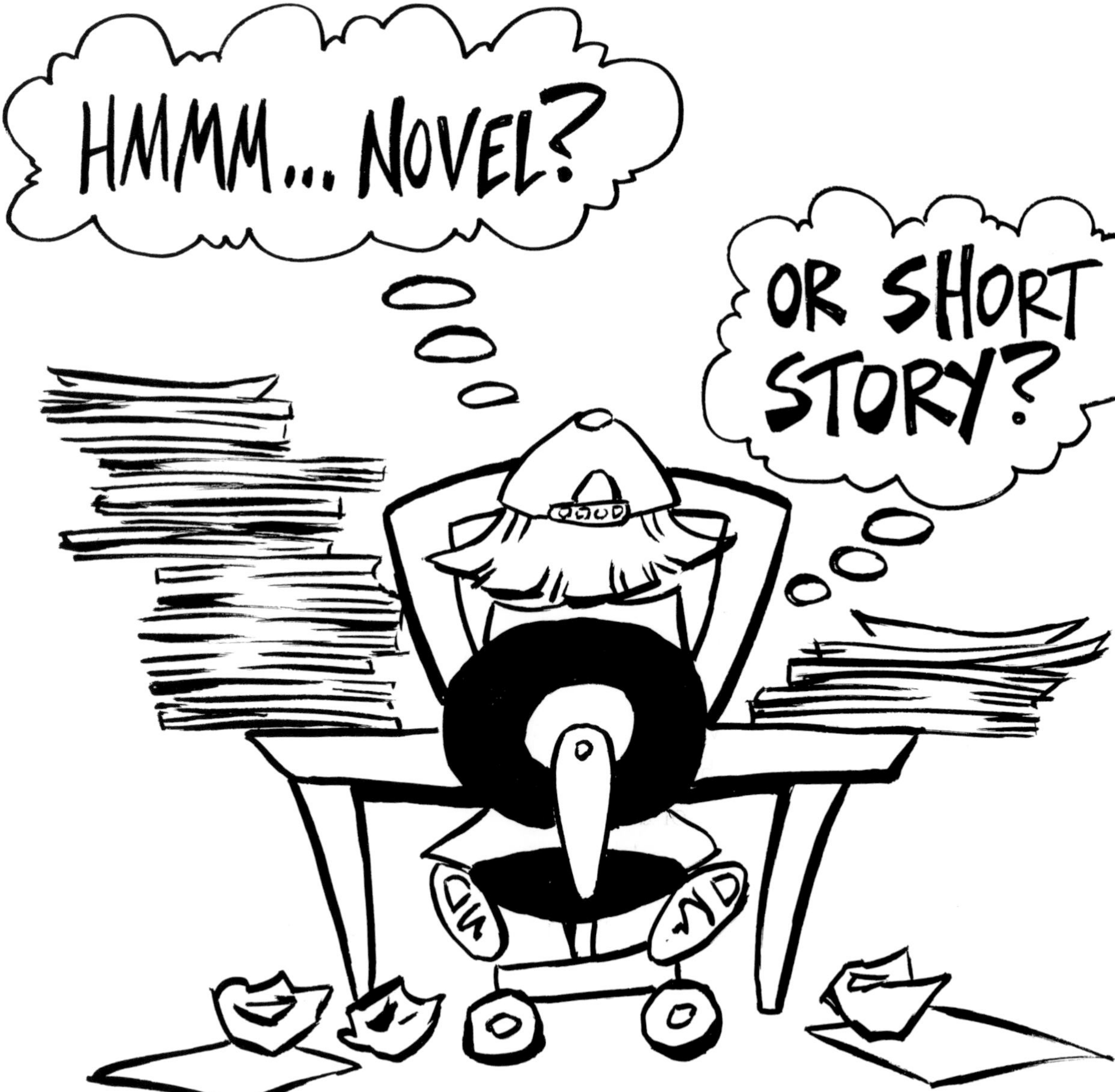
HMMM... NOVEL?
OR SHORT STORY?

CHAPTER 2

Fiction

THE SHORT STORY

Short stories have been around for thousands of years. In the Middle Ages, short stories were fables with a moral at the end. In the nineteenth century, writer Edgar Allan Poe developed some rules for the short story. He thought that every paragraph, sentence, and word must be designed to have a single effect on the reader.

SHORT STORY

A short story has a feeling of immediacy. It happens in the present but gives a hint of the past and a glimpse of the future. In order to do this with so few words, the short story has to be well structured. Chances are that while you probably love to read novels, you don't have the time to write one. But you do have the time to write a short story. How do short stories and novels differ?

The difference between novels and short stories is length and focus. Novels average over 50,000 words, or approximately 200 manuscript pages. Short stories are generally no more than 1,500 to 10,000 words, ranging from about 6 to 40 double-spaced pages.

Think of a novel as a family photo album with many characters, locations, and histories. A short story is a single photograph taken from that album showing a brief moment in a person's life. The short story focuses on the character's relationship to the world in a particular place and time.

STRUCTURE

The basic fiction story form is to have a beginning, middle, and end. Because short stories have a limited amount of words, you have less time and space to tell your story. Here is a simple way to structure a short story.

Create a list of all the events that are going to happen in the story. Put them in sequence as they occur.

Let's use Chris's story to illustrate this.

1. Chris wants to impress his father.
2. His father is too busy to spend time with Chris.
3. Chris decides to try out for the football team.
4. His father reminisces about being the captain of his football team.
5. Chris suffers a minor injury during the first scrimmage.
6. The coach counsels Chris to improve his strength by weight lifting.
7. Chris decides to take steroids to improve his performance.
8. Chris suffers dizziness during practice.
9. The coach notices Chris's physical changes.
10. Chris's best friend accuses him of drug use and warns him about health effects.

Continue the list until you have outlined all the events in the story.

Now you have a list of the things that will happen in the story. But not every event is worthy of being developed into a scene. Most short stories have approximately six scenes. What do you do with the leftover events? You can use them as transitions. A **transition** is a bridge from one scene to another. It can summarize the passage of time or a change of setting.

In the young athlete story, the father reminiscing about being the captain of the football team could be a bridge to a new scene.

Last night at dinner, Dad put his cell phone down long enough to tell me how he captained his football team during his junior year. As if I didn't feel bad enough.

Now determine which scenes will best tell your story. In a short story the beginning section should have no more than two scenes and a plot point. The middle part of your story can contain three or four scenes that show complications and obstacles. Plot point two will propel the main character into the most dramatic scene in the story, the climax. After the climax will come the final scene, which is the end of the story.

SHORT-SHORT STORY

The short-short story is 1,500 words or less and built on a theme rather than a complex plot. You have a very limited number of words to show characterization, conflict, and resolution.

Think of it as writing on a postcard, where you have a tiny amount of space in which to tell the story. Use as few characters and scenes as possible. Only the protagonist's attitude can change. The reader knows that this change will alter the character's outlook on life.

A writer of short-short stories must weave a tale by *showing* instead of *telling*. The goal is to create a picture so that the reader can see what the writer sees. With a few well-placed action verbs the writer paints a picture of a character and what he is feeling. For instance, "Uncle Joe is tired" *tells* us what Uncle Joe is feeling, while "Uncle Joe yawned, leaned back, and closed his eyes" *shows* how tired he is.

WRITING EXERCISES

Rewrite these sentences to *show* rather than *tell*.

1. The man is happy.
2. The little girl is angry.
3. The house is scary.
4. The dog is big.
5. The sandwich is good.

Like novels, short stories come in many different genres. You can write mystery, fantasy, science fiction, humor, or stories for television and film, for example.

Magazines are always looking for short stories to fill their pages each month, and e-zines need stories to fill their electronic pages. For young authors, it is more realistic to write and sell a 1,500-word short story than to complete a 50,000-word novel. By focusing on a specific short-story genre, you will increase your chances of being published. Let's explore the different kinds of genres you can write.

CHAPTER 3

Mystery

FROM SLEUTH TO SPY

The word "mystery" comes from the Greek word *mysterion*, which means "to keep silent." In modern mysteries the main character spends most of the story trying to get information from people who have secrets. Readers enjoy the suspense of trying to figure out "Who did it?" long before the final page.

The modern mystery has its roots in the medieval morality play. In this type of play, characters represent positive ideas such as generosity, kindness, and faith or negative concepts such as pride, laziness, and envy. Today, mystery writers use the private detective or amateur sleuth to show positive characteristics such as honesty, humor, and wit while loading down the villain with negative traits such as greed, deceit, and lust. There are many types of mystery stories.

TYPES OF MYSTERY STORIES

Amateur Sleuth

The amateur sleuth has no connection with the police and therefore doesn't follow their rules to get to the bottom of a crime. He or she is usually a curious individual who has been pulled into a mystery by a friend or an event. Amateur sleuths use their brains, powers of observation, and knowledge of the world to solve the mystery.

Matthew's new babysitting job looked like a piece of cake. It was nine o'clock on a Saturday, the Baker twins were sound asleep, and he had two more hours to watch his favorite movie and raid the refrigerator. It was the perfect babysitting job…until he heard the back door open.

Cozy

The cozy crime solver is also an amateur but usually a female. She is sophisticated about life and a good observer of people. Cozies often take place in rural settings where people are wealthy and live in large houses. These mysteries focus on character relationships and underplay the violence of crime.

Miss Wordwell sighed as she put the last dusty volume of Shakespeare back on the library shelf. It was the end of a very long day. She looked forward to a quiet weekend of reading sonnets and playing with her cat, Hamlet. Then she noticed that the house across the street had an unfamiliar car parked in the driveway. What made it more interesting was that the driver was obviously dead.

Private Detective

The private detective or investigator is usually a loner who works by him- or herself. The main character has a tough and cynical exterior but a strong internal sense of right and wrong. The story is often told from the first-person point of view. These mysteries are fast-paced, filled with action, and generally set in a large city.

Why does it always rain on my night off? I hate this city, especially in February. This case I'm working on is going nowhere and the client who hired me obviously lied. But my sense of duty gets the better of me, especially since I've spent his money and the guy is dead.

Police Procedural

Here the crime solver works for the police department. He or she knows correct law enforcement procedures and uses scientific techniques to solve the crime. In this type of mystery, the story focuses on the process of investigation rather than on the main character.

As far as Amelia was concerned, Sergeant McDowell had it in for her. He didn't appreciate criminal psychology and thought her degree wasn't worth the paper it was printed on. But even he had to be impressed when Amelia came up with a profile of the person who had the nerve to steal a million-dollar painting right off the mayor's living-room wall. Now all she had to do was convince McDowell that the thief was the mayor's grandmother.

Romantic or Historic

The romantic or historical mystery is usually set in the past, and generally the main character is a woman. There is a strong element of romance throughout the story. At its conclusion, the heroine and hero end up together. Use of flowery description is common in this type of story.

Glennis touched the gold brooch at her long slender throat. Her red hair glistened in the candlelight. Where was he? Alfred had promised to return at dusk, but it was late and the candle burned low in her bedroom alcove. Suddenly she heard the sound of distant thunder... or perhaps it was the beating of her heart.

Thrillers or Spy Stories

In the traditional thriller, the hero is not only trying to solve a mystery; he or she is trying to save the world. The emphasis is on good versus evil. The story takes place in exotic locations where the hero is in constant danger. He or she survives through risk-taking adventure and the use of high-tech weapons.

Clay Jordan cinched the clasp on his Super-Tex glove and brushed the snow from his gaiters. He knew the risks involved in climbing so late in the day. With only two hours of daylight left, the chance of getting down the mountain was remote. But somewhere on the cliff above was the airplane's black box. He had to find it before the Peruvian officials got there. He had to find it first.

There is a difference between stereotypes and character types. A stereotype feels like the same old clichéd character you've seen and read about time and again: the old cowboy, the damsel in distress. But when a writer crafts a distinct personality, characters become unique individuals.

While the mystery genre is filled with character types, your job as a writer is to create unique and memorable personalities within these types so that your reader can both easily identify the genre and read about exciting characters.

A good mystery story captures a reader's interest in the first paragraph and makes him or her want to read on. Mysteries and puzzles have a lot in common. Both present a problem that has to be solved.

Ideas

Ideas for mysteries can come from everyday events. Keep a notebook of potential ideas from newspaper articles, TV shows, books you've read, or personal experiences.

PoliceBeat

NORTHGLEN POLICE ARE SEARCHING FOR A MAN WHO ENTERED LUCKY's CONVENIENCE STORE ON WEDNESDAY MORNING AND RAN OFF WITH AN UNDISCLOSED AMOUNT OF BEEF JERKY.

HE IS DESCRIBED AS 5'9" WITH A THIN BUILD DRESSED IN A PLAID SUIT. HE WAS ALSO WEARING A CLOWN NOSE AND CARRYING A MINIATURE DACHSUND.

Plot

Mystery stories are more dependent on strong logic than any other genre. When you are writing a mystery, it is crucial to outline your story. A mystery writer begins with an answer and works backward to create the question. Something has happened. For instance, there's been a burglary. Who did it? Why did they do it?

You can create an outline scene by scene, letting the events build and build. Or you can jot down short notes that list the characters and their actions and reactions. Many mystery writers write the ending first. Play fair with your readers and arrange your facts so that they add up to a satisfying conclusion.

In writing your mystery, aim to have the readers know the setting, crime, victim, and sleuth by the end of the second page. In the middle of the story introduce clues and suspects and their motivations. Build suspense and danger until the climax of the story. The story should end after the most dramatic moment when all the facts are presented, all the suspects are eliminated, the villain is revealed, and the mystery is solved.

Setting

The first thing you have to decide is where your mystery will take place. Settings add mood and suspense to the story. Put your story in a place that lends atmosphere and color to your mystery. If you choose to set your story in the past or in a city you're unfamiliar with, you'll have to do research.

Involve all five senses to add sounds, tastes, smells, sights, and feelings. Show your readers the eerie light on the tombstone and let them feel the cold metal of the gun; don't just tell them about it.

Visit the location and take notes. Even your backyard can become a mysterious place after sunset. Add weather: the sound of rain beating against the roof or the sound of the wind ripping at the bedroom shutters.

Characters

Your main character will determine the type of mystery you write. If you choose a loner, you will probably want to write a private detective or spy mystery. If you choose an everyday person who is outside the police field, you will probably create an amateur detective mystery. Make your main character, or protagonist, so interesting that your readers will be cheering for him or her throughout the story.

The villain, or antagonist, has to be developed as clearly as the main character. The villain should be introduced early in the story and must have a motive. The most common motive for crime is self-interest: greed, jealousy, or revenge.

Avoid stereotypes. Give the villain enough good qualities to keep him or her human in order for your reader to understand the underlying motivation or behavior, but don't make the villain more interesting or sympathetic than your main character. You don't want your readers rooting for the bad guy.

Minor or secondary characters provide readers with facts and information about the crime. They are also potential suspects. Secondary characters should also be realistic and not stereotypes. Use unusual names, dialogue, and clever descriptions so that readers can see them as distinct personalities.

Every mystery story has to have a group of suspects who could have committed the crime. The main character or hero is the one who will tell the story through the first- or third-person point of view.

Clues

As soon as your detective discovers the crime, he or she will start looking for clues. Your detective follows the trail of clues by asking questions. Were there any witnesses? Were there footprints? Did someone have a key? Why was the suspect wearing a clown nose? Clues are separate pieces of information that, when fitted together, help your main character solve the crime. Clues can spice up scenes by introducing minor characters, adding suspense, and sharpening focus.

Sprinkle clues throughout the story, making each clue lead to a new suspect or a new plot twist. The easiest sort of clue to add is a lie or a statement that reveals knowledge an innocent suspect couldn't have. Clues reveal one of the following essentials in mysteries: motive (why the crime was done), opportunity (when it was done), or means (how it was done).

MOTIVE: WHY DID THE VILLAIN COMMIT THE CRIME?
OPPORTUNITY: WHEN DID HE COMMIT THE CRIME?
MEANS: HOW DID HE COMMIT THE CRIME?

Clues that lead readers in a false direction are called **red herrings.** The original red herring was a smoked fish with a strong odor. It was dragged across a trail to distract hunting hounds. In a mystery story, the distraction may be a false lead or piece of information that takes your detective off the true trail of the crime. Red herrings are designed to make the job of solving the mystery more difficult. A character with a motive and opportunity for the crime who turns out not to be the perpetrator is said to be a red herring. But remember to play fair with your readers. No clues should be left dangling. If you use red herrings, they should all be explained by the time the mystery is solved.

Suspense

Every mystery story should have a strong element of suspense. **Suspense** is a feeling of danger that makes readers anxious about the outcome of the story. To have readers sitting on the edge of their seats, you must create a feeling of danger for the main character. Do the unexpected. Add surprises to keep your readers guessing.

Writers use a fast-paced plot, compelling characters, and a careful choice of names to create suspense. A character named Darth Vader, for example, is more ominous and dangerous-sounding than Dennis Vader. Give your main character a limited amount of time to solve the mystery. When the hero has only minutes to free himself before the bomb explodes, you have successfully added suspense.

Solution

Once all your clues are in place, the main character is close to solving the crime. This is the climax, the most dangerous or exciting point in the story. It comes from all the events that have gone before. The climax is the turning point in the story's action.

The solution to the mystery has to be logical and arise out of the facts and clues the main character has discovered. Once the sleuth brings all the evidence to the readers' attention, the solution should be obvious. It must explain the villain's motive, opportunity, and means.

WRITING EXERCISES

1. You're writing the beginning of a mystery story involving an amateur sleuth. Write two scenes introducing the main character and the crime.
2. Develop two suspects, one male and one female. Give each a motive for committing the crime.
3. Write a paragraph using an abandoned shopping mall as the setting. Use plenty of sensory details and images.
4. Practice writing dialogue. Use the amateur sleuth and one of the suspects to reveal an important clue.
5. Write a suspenseful scene in which your amateur sleuth is in danger. Make it the climax of your story.

CHAPTER 4

Speculative Fiction

SCIENCE FICTION AND FANTASY

On Halloween night, 1938, Americans gathered around their radios as the announcer shouted:

Good heavens, something's wriggling out of the shadow like a gray snake. Now it's another one, and another. They look like tentacles to me. There, I can see the thing's body. It's large as a bear, and it glitters like wet leather. But the face—it's indescribable...

Everyone thought Martians were conquering Earth with heat rays and superweapons. Radio audiences, thinking that the events described in the broadcast were real, ran screaming into the streets. The next day the broadcasting company apologized for the "performance" of author H. G. Wells's *The War of the Worlds*. But for science fiction, the event was a turning point. Soon seven new science fiction magazines were up and running.

About the same time in England, J. R. R. Tolkien, a professor at Oxford University, was creating a series of fantasy books about Middle-earth, a world inhabited by elves, ogres, and hobbits. His book *The Hobbit* was followed by *The Lord of the Rings*, a classic fantasy series.

Today both science fiction and fantasy fall under the umbrella of the speculative fiction genre. Speculative fiction embraces many things: imaginative creatures, fantastic worlds, alien adventures, horrific monsters, fairy tales, and talking animals.

Science is at the core of science fiction, while magic lies at the heart of fantasy. In science fiction, the story is based on scientific law. In fantasy, there are no such laws. Science fiction predicts the future: the development of space travel, men on the moon, artificial intelligence. Fantasy reflects the past with a magical eye: the beauty of unicorns, the fierceness of dragons, the magic of sorcerers.

SCIENCE FICTION

Scholars tell us that the first true science fiction story was written by the Greek Lucian of Samosata about 175 A.D. In his story, a sailing ship is borne aloft by a great whirlwind and carried to the moon.

The direct ancestors of modern science fiction are Mary Shelley's *Frankenstein* and Jules Verne's 20,000 *Leagues Under the Sea*.

Today's science fiction emphasizes the effects of science and technology on people. Since science is so important in writing science fiction, accuracy of scientific facts is essential. As in other genres, there are many subcategories of science fiction.

TYPES OF SCIENCE FICTION

Hard Science Fiction

These stories are usually based on "hard science" where existing technologies have been projected to their logical conclusion in the future. Writers must do a lot of research to get the science right. 20,000 *Leagues Under the Sea* is a classic example of hard science fiction. Jules Verne predicted a world that would use submarines to explore the deepest mysteries of the ocean years before it happened.

John Stith bases his story *Red Shift Rendezvous* on the science of the movement of light. And Charles Sheffield's book *Starfire* is set in a space colony.

Space Opera

In these science fiction stories, characters are drawn in broad strokes of good and evil. The characters are larger than life, and the stories are highly dramatic and full of action. This subgenre is often thought of as an adventure or western story set in space, where good guys beat out bad guys. Examples of this genre are *Star Wars* and the *Star Trek* series.

Alternate History

Time travel is a common theme used in alternate history, where the main character moves backward or forward in time. This movement may or may not effect changes in history, depending on the rules that the writer establishes. The stories *Singularity* by William Sleator and A *Swiftly Tilting Planet* by Madeleine L'Engle illustrate such journeys through space and time.

Cyperpunk

These stories take place in the near future and involve an underdog protagonist who battles against big institutions or an unfeeling government. In cyberpunk the future is bleak. Here human beings and computers are on intimate terms. Chips are attached to human brains, creating a world that is impersonal, dangerous, and chaotic.

In William Gibson's book *All Tomorrow's Parties*, the action takes place in a San Francisco that has been torn apart by a recent earthquake. A misfit detective attempts to save the world from a cataclysmic paradigm shift. A paradigm is a model or pattern. The phrase "paradigm shift" is used in speculative fiction to describe the moment that a character experiences a rapid change in perspective. This dramatic shift results in the character and the story moving in a new, exciting direction.

Military Science Fiction

These science fiction stories revolve around futuristic military warfare. Highly sophisticated military technology is created in the battle of good against evil.

Authors of military science fiction are keenly interested in the latest military technology and expand these ideas into the war machines of tomorrow. One of the classics in this genre is Orson Scott Card's book *Ender's Game*, a coming-of-age science fiction story in which a brilliant young protagonist is trained in an artificial military environment.

FANTASY

Fantasy stories are as old as fairy tales, legends, and myths. They take place in a world where trees speak, animals fly, and transformation is an everyday occurrence. The language of fantasy is more poetic and literary in style than the language in the hard-edged technological world of science fiction. The conflicts and struggles of fantasy must be a matter of life and death. The main characters succeed because of their simple human characteristics, such as love, loyalty, and perseverance. Good fantasy writers know how to offer a moral while telling a good story.

Ancient Greek myths, the stories of Hans Christian Andersen, and *The Jungle Book* by Rudyard Kipling are some of the forerunners of modern fantasy writing.

TYPES OF FANTASY

High Fantasy
The world of high fantasy is peopled with elves, dwarves, trolls, kings, knights, and dragons. This ancient world is characterized by

codes of honor and a love of tradition. Here characters journey to distant lands on heroic quests to win a prize or save the world. Of all the types of fantasy, high fantasy is the most poetic in form. *The Lord of the Rings* by J. R. R. Tolkien and the stories of Jane Yolen and T. A. Barron are all examples of high fantasy.

Comic Fantasy

Comic fantasies can be about talking animals, tiny people, and humorous characters. In these stories, the characters' playfulness and sense of the ridiculous are as important as the magic. The style is light and funny. Examples include *Charlotte's Web* by E. B. White and the Harry Potter books by J. K. Rowling.

Dark Fantasy

Evil characters and the world of the supernatural are the ingredients of dark fantasy. Horror stories with frightening magic and scary creatures populate this underworld. The hero is often faced with his own fears and negative traits before he can conquer the evil antagonist. Good examples of dark fantasy are Clive Barker's *The Thief of Always* and Paul Zindel's *Doomstone*.

Realistic Fantasy

In these stories, everyday characters have their lives turned upside down by one magical event. Once enchanted, the characters voluntarily participate in events that will change them forever and ultimately take them home. Authors of these stories work hard to present a realistic world with magic seeping through the cracks. Good examples of realistic fantasy are *Princess in the Pigpen* by Jane Resh Thomas, *The Indian in the Cupboard* by Lynne Reid Banks, and *Tuck Everlasting* by Natalie Babbitt.

A STEP-BY-STEP GUIDE TO BUILDING YOUR SPECULATIVE FICTION WORLD

Before you create your speculative fiction story or introduce your characters, visualize and create a world with its own set of rules. Without a believable and compelling world, your story and characters will never be convincing to the reader.

Your Speculative Fiction World

Picture your setting. Is it a planet or a kingdom? What kind of climate does it have: hot and dry or cold and icy? Are there active volcanoes or ancient mountains? Think about possible creatures or animals and the things they need to survive. What are the life cycles and what are the sources of food?

Intelligent Creatures

In most cases you want intelligent creatures or perceptive life forms in your world. Decide what your creatures look like and what they resemble in our world. If you use human creatures, make sure their life-style reflects the rules of their world. An example is Janet Taylor Lisle's book *Forest*, in which the squirrels live in the upper forest and the humans live in the lower forest. Each area has its own inhabitants and rules.

I Never Met an Alien I Didn't Like

An alien or nonhuman character will be all the more real if it has familiar aspects that readers know and like. An alien who loves his family and is loyal to friends is someone or something readers can identify with.

As in other fiction, your creature must have a history. Add as many details in the history of your character as you can think of.

Use specific character flaws such as greed, jealousy, or laziness to make your alien more realistic. If the alien is boastful or the android is insecure, know why they are that way. Let their personalities come from their histories. And if the alien has a special nature or ability, let your readers know.

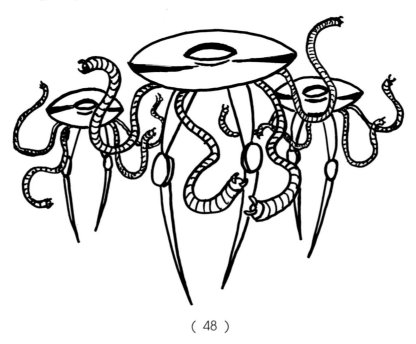

History

Once you have created interesting creatures or intelligent life forms, your world needs a history. You could use something from the past to create a history for your planet or kingdom. An ancient scroll or a buried time capsule might reveal historical artifacts that explain the current conflict in your world.

Who or what rules your world? A benevolent king or a heartless computer? What are the goals and dreams of the inhabitants of your world? How have the inhabitants been repressed and what will they do in the future? The history of your world will grow and develop as you work on your story, but for now sketch out the major points and stick to them.

Religion and Magic

Religion is often connected with history and can be a key point of conflict. Is there only one system of belief tolerated in your world? Does the world have one religion or many?

If your speculative fiction tale has more fantasy elements than science, you may want to create a full-blown magic system and a code of ethics. Anything is possible—just spell out the rules of who can do what and why.

Culture

Create unique activities for your world, such as singing, dancing, painting, or sports. Remember that your world's culture should be related to your creatures' deepest yearnings. For instance, in the Harry Potter books, the young wizards-in-training spend their free time playing Quidditch, a game that emphasizes keen eyesight and quick reflexes.

PUTTING IT ALL TOGETHER

Once you have sketched out your ideas for a physical world of intelligent creatures with a history, religion, code of ethics, and culture, put them all together. Write a descriptive paragraph about your world.

How did the physical features of your world affect its history? How did its history affect its religion? And finally, how does the culture of your world reflect all of the above?

WRITING EXERCISES

For the following exercises, choose either science fiction or fantasy.

1. Think about your world. This is the setting of your story. Write two paragraphs that describe what your house would look like in this world.
2. Create a main character and have him, her, or it describe him-, her-, or itself by looking in a mirror.
3. Sum up your main character's problem in three sentences. Who will become the antagonist and what will become the obstacle?
4. Create a list of all the events that will happen in your story.
5. Using the short story form, identify six or seven scenes you will use to dramatize your story.

CHAPTER 5

Writing for the Screen

TELEVISION AND FILM

Whenen was the last time you watched a movie or your favorite television series? Did you ever wonder how the actors in *Star Wars*, *Jurassic Park*, or *Tarzan* knew what to say or what to do? Behind every good movie or television show is a great script. Screenwriters create an imaginary visual world for the "small screen" of television or the "big screen" of movies.

(51)

People who write for these visual genres are called **screenwriters** and the scripts they write are called **screenplays**.

Fiction writers use strong action verbs, specific details, figures of speech, and powerful descriptions to pull readers into their imaginary worlds. Screenwriters use directors, actors, camera people, and special effects to project their imaginary worlds onto the screen.

For hundreds of years writers have written scripts for the stage. These plays were the forerunners of modern film and television. A screenplay is a writing genre where words are secondary to visual images.

Before you begin to write a screenplay, you must have an idea or **premise**. The premise contains a basic plot with a beginning, middle, and end. Once you have an idea, create a **treatment**, or narrative outline, by writing details about the plot, characters, and action without using dialogue.

The screenplay uses a three-act dramatic structure. Act one is the beginning, or setup; act two is the middle, or confrontation; and act three is the end, or resolution. Television screenplays use a six-act dramatic structure in which each act is divided into two scenes.

When you write a screenplay, there is a specific form that your script must follow. One page of a screenplay is the equivalent of one minute of screen time. Most full-length feature films are about 120 minutes long. This means that the scripts for these films are 120 pages long.

When you first begin to practice writing a screenplay, try a ten-minute movie, or ten pages of script. Later, after you have more practice with the screenwriting format, you can expand the length of your screenplay.

ACT ONE: THE SETUP

In act one of a screenplay, you introduce the setting, characters, situation, and relationships among the characters. Create a dramatic question that can be answered with a simple yes or no. Will the boy get the girl? Will the lost dog find its way home? Will the hero escape from the space station before the villain blows it up?

Within the first ten minutes of the movie, the viewer must know who the main character is and what his or her goal is. This will take approximately ten pages of your script. For your first practice screenplay, write three pages.

ACT TWO: THE CONFRONTATION

Act two is the middle of your screenplay and shows dramatic conflict through confrontation. The hero must meet a series of obstacles as he strives to achieve his goal. Things need to happen to keep your audience interested. All drama is conflict. Create barriers or roadblocks for your hero to overcome.

In this section of your screenplay, you must develop and answer these questions:

What must the hero do to achieve his goal?
What difficulties will the hero confront?
What motivates your hero to keep going?

A real screenplay designates about sixty pages to the middle or confrontation section. In your short version, write five pages.

The last thirty pages of a screenplay are called act three, or the resolution. In this section you must find a solution to your hero's quest. Answer all the questions that you have created for your main character. This is the part of the screenplay when the boy gets the girl, the dog arrives home, and the villain is defeated. In act three, tie up all the loose threads and find an ending for the story. In your practice version, write your ending in two pages.

PLOT POINTS

To transition between these three acts, screenwriters use **plot points**. As with fiction, a plot point is any incident, episode, or event that spins the action in a new direction. Until this moment the audience thought the boy would meet the girl of his dreams, the dog was headed home, and the spaceship was traveling around the galaxy.

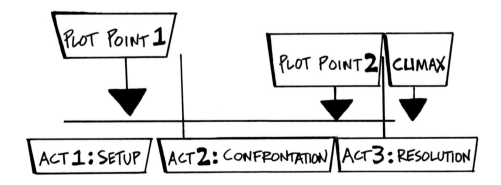

At the first plot point in act one, the boy arrives too late to meet the girl, the traveling dog meets up with a friendly badger, and the villain manages to climb aboard the spaceship to plant a bomb. All three of these plot points push your story in a new direction.

The focus of act two is conflict. The main character must deal with increasingly complicated problems. At the end of act two, the second plot point is another major decision for the main character. This decision pushes the protagonist into the climax, the highest dramatic moment in the story. For example, the girl thinks the boy isn't coming and decides to marry someone else, the dog hurts its leg, and the villain activates the bomb.

SCENES

Acts are made up of a series of scenes. As in fiction, each scene should have a purpose. Well-written scenes show a specific time and place, move the story along by showing conflict between characters, and pass on vital information to the audience.

SCREENPLAY FORMAT

When you write a screenplay, you must learn some basic movie-making vocabulary. No one expects you to be a cinematographer, but you have to be able to visualize what's happening on screen. The form of the screenplay includes character names, stage directions, scene locations, dialogue, special effects, and music.

Screenplays are typed in a specific format. Here's a short scene written in screenplay format.

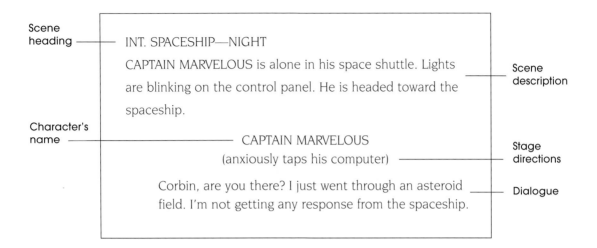

Scene heading —— INT. SPACESHIP—NIGHT

CAPTAIN MARVELOUS is alone in his space shuttle. Lights are blinking on the control panel. He is headed toward the spaceship. —— Scene description

Character's name ——

CAPTAIN MARVELOUS
(anxiously taps his computer) —— Stage directions

Corbin, are you there? I just went through an asteroid field. I'm not getting any response from the spaceship. —— Dialogue

The **scene heading** tells the location and the time of day. It is always written in capital letters. The abbreviation INT. tells the camera person that an interior, or inside, camera location is required, while EXT. indicates an exterior, or outside, camera location.

The **scene description** conveys the visual aspect of the scene in as few words as possible.

The **character's name** indicates who is speaking and is capitalized and centered.

Stage directions are written in parentheses, centered, and single-spaced under the character's name. They give the actor hints about the character's actions and emotions.

Dialogue is placed in the center of the page and single-spaced under the character's name.

All stories must begin with compelling characters, and so must screenplays. The needs of your main character will provide you with the end of your story. Begin by thinking of the ending. Screenwriters have several ways of organizing their ideas before they begin to write.

1. **Card method.** Use index cards to organize your screenplay into three acts. Begin by describing a single scene on each card.

    Remember to add plot points at the end of act one and act two. In the example, the plot point for act one would be scene four. Determine the climax or most exciting scene and write that on a card. Use as many cards as you like. The advantage of using cards is that your scenes can easily be moved from act to act.

> FIDO WITH LOVING OWNER.

> OWNER AND FIDO GOING FOR A PICNIC.

> FIDO CHASES RABBIT.

> OWNER DRIVES OFF WITHOUT FIDO.

2. **Narrative method.** You may feel more comfortable by first writing your screenplay as a short story. Don't worry about descriptive language. Just get the story on paper. From here you can begin to write your story in screenplay format.

3. **Outline method.** Some writers prefer the outline method. Tell your story in short main headings, listing scenes and dialogue under each act.

WRITING EXERCISES

1. Choose a character and write a brief summary of his or her goals in life.
2. What roadblocks will he or she face?
3. Write a short dialogue between your main character and your villain.
4. Sketch your story into three acts. Where will the plot points and the climax be?
5. Write a short scene using correct screenplay format.

CHAPTER 6

HUMOR WRITING

TICKLING THE FUNNY BONE

Being funny is serious business. Writing humor is difficult because making people laugh isn't easy. The good news is that almost anything you can think of can be turned into something humorous.

You can write funny stories about famous people or your Aunt Mabel and Uncle Louie, about national events or the food in your cafeteria. In other words, almost nothing is sacred. The whole world and everything in it can be used as material for humor writing.

What is funny? People laugh at ideas and stories that have a twist or surprise, and punchlines that don't need an explanation.

Try looking at everyday experiences in unusual ways. What would your family dog say about its life? What if you were in charge of all the television programming at your house? What would you make your parents watch, and why? If you had to write a new set of rules for teenage party etiquette, what would they be?

The key to being funny is to push your work to the brink but not over the edge. Not everybody has the same sense of humor. Use good taste and judgment. Think about the audience and decide what's right for them. If you were the reader, would you find your writing funny or in poor taste?

THE SIX TYPES OF HUMOR

Light humor is humor that pokes fun at human weaknesses.

My dad truly believes that he can play steel guitar and that any day now Bruce Springsteen will be calling to ask him to play backup.

Irony involves saying exactly what you don't mean.

Aren't toothaches fun?

Exaggeration describes an everyday event and overstates the way people react to it.

The lunches in the cafeteria are so bad that my best friend brought his dog to school to be his food taster.

Satire is a literary technique that makes fun of powerful or influential people, institutions, or trends. It is difficult to write because the writer takes a serious and timely subject such as race relations, school violence, or the high cost of college and pokes fun at it. *Mad* magazine is filled with social satire.

Parody is an imitation of a song, story, or movie plot that uses a different subject. For instance, take the familiar "Happy Birthday" tune, change the subject, and you've created a parody.

Off-the-wall humor looks at ordinary life from an unusual perspective. Try to describe a typical Monday morning at your house from your cat's point of view.

ELEMENTS OF HUMOR

One way to learn what is funny is to read the works of *humorists,* or people who write humor. Compare your humor to the works of others. The more you read and write humor, the funnier you will become.

Choose a writer whom you find funny and try to imitate his or her writing. Study the work as a whole. Find the writer's sense of pacing, rhythm, and tempo. Notice the style of the writing. Is it tight and clean? Or does it ramble from subject to subject?

Start by observing everyday things and recording your observations. Try to capture in words what you are passionate about; then add the humorous twist. Detail what is true for you and then poke fun at yourself. Describe your own weaknesses, frustrations, or fears by using exaggeration, comical situations, or funny dialogue.

Many times humor fails because the writer goes on too long or forgets the main point of the story. Some wandering is good and often funny when you are talking to your friends. But on paper the words must be clear, descriptive, and well chosen to be entertaining.

Look for patterns of humor. Examine the beginning paragraph and look for the writer's theme or point of view. Most humor writers present a narrow idea at first and then go off in various directions as the piece goes on:

Let's do away with Mondays. They're a waste of time. Nobody wants to get up for them after the weekend. It's the one day of the week that has a really bad reputation. After all, who wants to do anything on a day that's associated with the words "blue" or "blah." We're not alone; people around the world hate Mondays in every language and in all cultures where people have to get out of bed.

Another element of humor is a false claim or exaggeration:

Substitute teachers are an alien species. I believe that Mulder and Scully have it all wrong. Instead of looking for extraterrestrials who fly spaceships, they should be investigating the substitute teachers who drive dented little Hondas into our school parking lot.

You can also express humor through contradiction:

I think everybody over forty should take up skateboarding. After they break their legs, arms, and ankles, the sidewalks will be empty. Once we get rid of all those grumpy old people, we can return sidewalks to what they should be used for—skateboarding.

Use references that are familiar to your readers, such as music, television shows, movies, and celebrities. These specific references can elaborate an idea or emphasize a point. But resist throwing in too many extra details or funny asides. Don't try to make every line funny. It isn't necessary. Use only your best material.

Stand-up comics develop pacing and timing by performing in front of an audience. You need the same kind of training. Read your manuscript aloud and get some feedback from people you trust. Listen to it to find out if you are really funny! Humor is like poetry. You must develop an ear for it.

HUMOR FORMAT

There are various formats for humor writing, including columns, essays, poetry, short stories, books, greeting cards, gag lines, and of course puns and jokes.

COLUMNS AND ESSAYS

Humor columns and essays run anywhere from 500 words to 1,200 words. Newspapers usually want 650 words, while magazines will accept articles as long as 850 words. Writing a humor column requires a certain flow, like dancing or surfing. You can learn the steps by reading and studying other humor writers, but your own style and ease will come only with practice.

POETRY

Poet Shel Silverstein, author of *Where the Sidewalk Ends*, was a master at exaggerating everyday situations, like a messy room or taking out the garbage, to the point of hilarity.

Funny poetry is enjoyed more for its cleverness than its deep meaning. It often comes in four lines with a twist ending, but can be as long as twelve lines. Add a good rhyming dictionary to your library shelf to help you create funny verse.

> The two spots
> That I wish would match
> Are where I itch
> And where you scratch.
> —Joy C. Hulme

SHORT STORIES AND BOOKS

Humorous short story collections like Louis Sacher's *Wayside Stories from Sideways School* and *Never Cry Arp!* by Patrick McManus feature authors using everyday life to make a humorous or satirical point.

GREETING CARDS

Greeting cards are divided into two categories, cards that can be sold year-round and seasonal cards. Usually a card consists of a one-sentence setup on the front of the card with a short punch line inside. Greeting card companies are always looking for writers who can write short, tight, humorous verse. Spend time at your local

greeting card store and read the types of cards that are being published. Do your jokes and one-liners fit into their style and format?

JOKES, GAGS, PUNS

A **joke** is a story with a humorous or surprise ending. This ending is called the **punchline**. That's why a joke is seldom as funny the second time around: You know the ending.

A joke can be a **gag**, which is a brief, humorous statement that inspires a comical response. Gags are often referred to as "one-liners." A joke can also be a **pun**, where a word or words sound alike but have different meanings, such as "hair" and "hare."

There once was a red-haired man named Rudolph who spent every day watching the clouds go by and studying the weather. One morning a little girl passed by and said, "Rudolph, it looks like it's going to snow."

"No," said Rudolph, "it's going to rain!" He pointed up at the black clouds and said, "Rudolph the Red knows rain, dear."

1. Write a short column about the five lessons you can learn about life from watching professional wrestling.
2. Write a four-line humorous poem about your feet.
3. Create a birthday greeting card for your girlfriend's mother.
4. Make up a pun. It is really important that everybody groans after they hear it.
5. Write a joke about getting braces.

CHAPTER 7

Marketing

Once you've written a story, screenplay, or humorous piece, it's time to think about publishing it for others to read. The library or bookstore is the place to begin your search for possible markets for your story. Think about the types of magazines that you like to read, and start there. Magazines and writing contests are always looking for young talent.

Look carefully at the covers of magazines. They give you clues about their readers. Is the person on the cover smiling directly at you, kicking a soccer ball, or working on a computer? Publishers know that readers identify with cover illustrations. They hope readers will be attracted to the cover, pick up the magazine, look through it, and buy it.

Check out the table of contents, which is found near the front of the magazine. Does the magazine publish short fiction? How much? What do the story titles tell you about the types of fiction the magazine is interested in publishing? You'll also find the name of the editor and the address of the publisher near the table of contents.

Another way to find out who's reading this magazine is by looking at the advertisements. Ads reflect the readership of a magazine.

If the ads show guys with pierced ears riding snowboards, this is probably not the magazine for your fantasy story.

It is more difficult for young writers to publish novels. The National Writer's Association (www.nationalwriters.com) sponsors novel-writing contests, but rarely do book publishers publish works by very young writers. You have a better chance of getting your story published by a magazine or an e-zine on the Internet.

TRADITIONAL MARKETS

There are two more ways to find specific market information. One is to write a publisher directly and ask for a set of writer's guidelines. The other way is to use one of the many available writer's market guides, which will direct you to a publisher or magazine that publishes in your chosen genre.

The Novel and Short Story Writer's Market is a good place to begin. This book gives valuable marketing tips and updated information as well as the names and addresses of publishers.

The annual *Writer's Market*, published by *Writer's Digest*, gives publisher guidelines and submission procedures for magazines, book publishers, and script buyers.

The Market Guide for Young Writers, written by Kathy Henderson, is updated regularly. This book is tailored especially for young people and gives magazine and newspaper market information.

All these guides and others can be found at your local bookstore or library.

MANUSCRIPT FORMAT

1. Always type your story double-spaced on 8½-by-11-inch white paper.
2. Use a paper clip to hold pages together. Do not staple.
3. On the first page in the upper left-hand corner, list your name, address, phone number, and E-mail address.
4. On the first page in the upper right-hand corner, type the approximate word count of the manuscript and the copyright symbol (©), followed by the year. (According to the U.S. Copyright Office at the Library of Congress, when you write your story down, it is automatically copyrighted.)
5. Do not number the first page.
6. Center the title in capital letters one-third of the way down on the first page.
7. Drop down four spaces and begin your story.
8. On every page after the first, include a heading with your last name and the page number in the upper left- or upper right-hand corner.

ONLINE MARKETS

The newest and most exciting place to publish is online. There are many Web sites, online publishers, and e-zines looking for young authors and their work. Here are just a few to check out.

Kid Stuff: **www.kidstuff.org/indexes/ps.html** A colorful site where you can submit poems, stories, and essays.

About.Com: **kidswriting.about.com/teens/kidswriting** Creative writing site for teens.

Stone Soup: **www.stonesoup.com** Online magazine publishing for students ages eight to thirteen.

TeensOnline: **www.teens-online.com/ezine** Teen magazine for online publishing.

Kid's Story: **www.kidstory.com** A fun and exciting place to enjoy stories and poetry.

Cyberkids: **www.cyberkids.com** A quarterly magazine by students ages nine to sixteen that features articles, fiction, and poetry. Writing contributions are welcome.

Midlink: **longwood.cs.ucf.edu/~MidLink** (case sensitive) A bimonthly magazine that links middle schools around the world. Contributions from students ages ten to fifteen are welcome.

Inkspot.com: **inkspot.com/young/crit** A Web site where writers eighteen and under are invited to send in their work for critique by other readers and writers.

Wicked4kids: **www.wicked4kids.com/popup.htm** A Web site filled with jokes, puzzles, and limericks. A place to publish your humorous writing.

Frodo's Notebook: **www.quill.net/frodo** An online collection of poetry and essays. If you are a writer between thirteen and nineteen years old, you may submit work to be considered for publication on this site.

TeenInk: **www.teenink.com** TeenInk is a printed monthly publication and an online weekly magazine, written entirely by teens for teens.

Merlyn's Pen: **www.merlynspen.com** Everyone in grades six to twelve (or home-school or international equivalent) may submit writing. Art is not considered.

The end of this book is just the beginning of your genre writing career. You now know the story structure for longer fiction, short stories, and the various types of genres. Just by reading and studying this book, you have increased your chances of getting your stories published.

Read as much as you can in the genre you enjoy, and practice writing every day. Share your writing with a trusted teacher or friend and don't give up. Some of your favorite writers spent years perfecting their craft before they reached the best-seller list. Good luck and good writing.

General Writing Books

Asher, Sandy. *But That's Another Story: Favorite Authors Introduce Popular Genres*. New York: Walker, 1996.

Bergstrom, Joan and Craig. *All the Best Contests for Kids*, 5th ed. Berkeley, CA: Tricycle Press, 1996.

Bernays, Anne, and Pamela Painter. *What If? Writing Exercises for Fiction Writers*. New York: HarperCollins, 1990.

Emerson, Connie. *The 30-Minute Writer: How to Write and Sell Short Pieces*. Cincinnati: Writer's Digest Books, 1993.

Giblin, James. *Writing Books for Young People*. Boston: The Writer, 1995.

Guthrie, A.B., Jr. *A Field Guide to Writing Fiction*. New York: HarperCollins, 1991.

Kress, Nancy. *Beginnings, Middles and Ends*. Cincinnati: Writer's Digest Books, 1993.

Noble, William. *The 28 Biggest Writing Blunders (And How to Avoid Them)*. Cincinnati: Writer's Digest Books, 1993.

Stahl, R. James. *Stories by Students: Ten Great Stories from the Pages of Merlyn's Pen*. Greenwich, RI: Merlyn's Pen, 1992.

Stevens, Carla. *A Book of Your Own: Keeping a Diary or Journal*. New York: Clarion Books, 1993.

Tobias, Ronald B. *20 Master Plots and How to Build Them*. Cincinnati: Writer's Digest Books, 1993.

Wigand, Mollie. *How to Write and Sell Greeting Cards, Bumper Stickers, Tee-shirts and Other Fun Stuff*. Cincinnati: Writer's Digest Books, 1992.

The Writer's Encyclopedia, 3rd ed. Cincinnati: Writer's Digest Books, 1996.

The Writer's Digest Guide to Good Writing. Cincinnati: Writer's Digest Books, 1994.

Short Story

Bickman, Jack M. *Writing the Short Story*: A Hands-on Program. Cincinnati: Writer's Digest Books, 1994.

Fredette, Jean M. *The Writer's Digest Handbook of Short Story Writing*, vol. 2. Cincinnati: Writer's Digest Books, 1991.

Mystery Writing

Grafton, Sue. *Writing Mysteries*: A Handbook by the Mystery Writers of America. Cincinnati: Writer's Digest Books, 1992.

Greenberg, Martin H. *Great Writers and Kids Write Mystery Stories*. New York: Random House, 1996.

Speculative Fiction

Bova, Ben. *The Craft of Writing Science Fiction That Sells*. Cincinnati: Writer's Digest Books, 1994.

Costello, Matthew J. *How to Write Science Fiction*. New York: Marlowe, 1995.

Screenplay Writing

Fields, Sid. *Screenplay*: The Foundations for Screenwriting. New York: Dell Publishing, 1994.

Green, Roger. *Writing Better Fantasy*. East Greenwich, RI: Merlyn's Pen, 1992.

HUMOR

Helitzer, Melvin. *Comedy Writing Secrets*. Cincinnati: Writer's Digest Books, 1997.

Marketing

Henderson, Kathy. *The Market Guide for Young Writers*: Where and How to Sell What You Write, 5th ed. Cincinnati: Writer's Digest Books, 1996.

INDEX